I0486388

Legal & Disclaimer

Contents

Introduction

Network Marketing should come natural to all of us, because at its core, the basic premise of this business strategy is to be sociable, meet people, and to be able to clearly express ideas. These are skills that most of us learned from an early age, abilities that we honed in grade school as we made friends over chocolate milk and recess breaks. Network Marketing as a business platform is really just beefing up and enhancing the innate socializing ability we human beings use continuously in our daily lives, it is taking all of our common social sense and translating it into business sense over a very narrow bandwidth of communication directed at one specific product, service, or goal.

Used as an intensive marketing approach, Network Marketing attends to the notion that you can create great business contacts by way of personal and online dialogue. This Networking is used to increase the awareness of a service and maximize business potential through these networked relationships. Networking is a proven business strategy that fosters the growth of colleagues, prospects customers and referrals. It is through the utilization of all of these contacts within our own personal network that leads down a linked chain, from the product to you, to your down-line distributors, who automatically work to promote and market your product for you.

These "down lines" can consist of huge corporations or your family, friends and neighbors. They are mainly just any networked group of individuals who are dedicated to get the word out for your product or service. The most common way to gain these down line distributors is through the most classic sense of network marketing, which is, "word of mouth". This word of mouth can occur on the street, on the phone, or over your Face Book page, however the word gets out, it is networked into a tangible benefit for your business.

Have you ever heard that the squeaky wheel gets the grease? Well, we have all figured out at one point in our life or another, that if we really want something in this life we can't be silent, we have to let people know what our intentions are and what we are trying to accomplish through some form of communication. Because the only place that silence will get us is absolutely nowhere. You have to expand and promote your product in order to get the notice and attention that you desire.

Network Marketing in a lot of ways is the great equalizer in business. Because you don't have to have a lot of education, you don't need a PHD in Macro Economics in order to start finding leads and referrals. And you don't need a lot of money to start a simple Face Book page to promote your services. What you really need is something that money can not buy, which is your enthusiasm, creativity, and social intelligence. These things are innate skills that anyone can utilize. With easily proven strategies, the capability is brought directly within your reach. In many ways Network Marketing not only evens the playing field, it brings the field directly to us.

Grab Your Free Marketing Materials Here

If you've been building a list, you should know that writing emails can be hard...

Especially when you want to write emails that convert to sales.

There is a super shortcut for you to make money online -- using proven emails (without you doing the writing).

There are 2 weeks of fill-in-the-blank emails you can use to promote any related internet marketing products you like! Put in your own affiliate links and earn all the commission.

Or use them to promote your own products.

Get the email templates set for free by clicking on the link below:

http://bit.ly/2kGOEDd

Chapter 1: Network Marketing – Separating The Wheat from The Chaff

When I was a kid I used to hate it when I got some kind of electronic toy or gizmo of some sort, was all excited about it, only to realize I couldn't do anything with it because the box says, "batteries not included". The device couldn't be operated unless I bought some additional component to get it to run properly. Many of the Network Marketing programs are the same way and a lot of them should come with a label that reads, "Pyramid's Not Included". Because many of the get rich quick marketing strategies being proposed fall flat on their face when you take out the pyramid scheme's that they are built upon.

Network Marketing in itself is a viable way to produce realistic business but you have to be able to differentiate the flawed and fraud from the real deal network marketing techniques that can boost your revenue with real sales. That's why a "direct sales bible" just would not be complete without the exercise of this task. Because as these scams evolve you have to remain vigilant to you don't unknowingly get hoodwinked with an absolute waste of time.

The fraudsters are ruthless in trying to suck people into their gimmick and even legitimate job sites like career builder are becoming absolutely flooded with what they term "management" trainee programs. I myself quite accidentally applied and attended a pseudo interview with one of these larks shortly after college. It was a position that fronted itself as some sort of management position for a rural outfitter type store. Being a recent grad in desperate need of a job, I thought "What the heck?", might as well try it, maybe management could open doors for me.

Upon my entry to that interview site though, the situation quickly evolved from what was supposed to be a one on one Q and A session for managerial position to some slick salesman herding me and 15 other people into a stuffy room where he began some sort of rehearsed presentation of fake earrings! Apparently the only thing I was going to be trained to manage was my own door to door peddling of these ugly knock off's of feminine accessory!

And then while I'm sitting back in a dazed and depressed stupor trying to figure out what bizarre world I had just been transferred two, I begin to see the pyramid take shape right before my eyes as the guy describes how we can all earn at least $500 bucks a month if we just fork over $200 up front to begin our "management" training. "Wait a minute" I asked myself, how in the world do you make money by having to pay money? This my friends is the essence of a pyramid scheme.

These guys cook up these loony scenarios to where you pay an entrance fee to joint their little marketing club and then after that you spend all of your time not selling the product, but trying to hook other people into joining the network and paying the same fee you did, which you get a percentage of. This is what you are managing, the absurd transfer of entrance fee's from person to person.

This is why these fraudulent pyramid gimmicks are also known by another name as ; "money transfer" schemes. Because the goofy products, whether it's vacuum cleaners, a set of worthless Tupper wear, or women's jewelry, the product is never the primary focus, the main objective is always to recruit more people to the scheme, these are the poor guys that wind up at the bottom of the pyramid and then have to turn around and trick others in order to gain their money back and scale the walls of the scheme. It really is a horrible scam. So how to you know real network marketing from the schemes?

For one thing, authentic network marketing will never ask you to pay an entrance fee up front. Real direct sales, network marketing is a about the distribution of a valid and marketable product directly to a viable target audience. The main purpose of authentic network marketing is using a network of contacts to get the word out about your service or product. It is the focus on building an expanding network of contacts for this distribution and brand recognition that is the key, not entrance fees.

The traditional Network Marketing model has you as the first direct distributor and then as you gain momentum you acquire other leads in your network who work as what is called a "down line", making additional sales and contacts from where you began at the center. Again, unlike a pyramid scheme, these legitimate contacts focus on selling your marketable product and not on obtaining ridiculous fees. Real Network Marketing is all about getting your product out there to the public, as efficiently and expeditiously as you possibly can. So think of this as just a word to the wise, and lets avoid these pyramid nightmares and embrace true and effective Network Marketing that will rock the socks off of your business world!

Chapter 2: Building True Connection with Your Target Audience

Just who is it that you are trying to reach? This should be the question on the tip of your tongue every time you are beginning a venture into Network Marketing. You have to know your target audience. You have to know who will be the most responsive to whatever product or service that you are trying to sell. And once your target audience is identified the next thing you are going to have to do is determine how in the world it is that you will reach this target audience. Are you going to give them a call? E-mail them? Friend them on Face Book or are you going to meet up with potential clients face to face? How will you approach your target?

The personal approach of face to face communication is referred to in the direct marketing world as "broadcast" communication. Borrowing an analogy from TV, this phrase is meant to convey the fact that you are sending a wide range of images and signals to your audience with a direct face to face approach. Whereas an over the phone or internet approach is utilizing a much narrower focus, which continuing the same media metaphor, is a more narrowcast of information like a radio broadcast, where most of the visual cues are not picked up on.

In the narrower bandwidth of communication the internet offers it can be very difficult to be able to gauge a networking strategy that is tailor fit to the attitudes and reactions of the other person at the end of that e-mail or blog post. But it is not impossible, it just requires a bit of adjustment. All you really need to do is follow their feedback, like a great detective the internet can offer you up several clues about your target audience's buying habits and preferences, you just have to put them together.

Once a pattern has been established, make your promotional efforts match this set of behavior. And since you are using such a narrow communication channel you should make your overtures toward clients as friendly as possible, even using a bit of good natured humor and examples of personal interest to fill in the missing blanks of information. Just don't overdo it, make all written communication to the point, and avoid too much wordiness, run on sentences and typos. Remember, this is your professional promo and you want it to stand out.

And when it comes to reaching out to clients over the phone, there is an application even more vital than Face Book that you need to master; your voice. You need to be confident with an upbeat inflection at all times when talking to potential leads over the phone. Because having a defeated, unsure, or apologetic attitude when marketing your ideas over the phone will get you absolutely nowhere. Because if you think you will get a sympathy card by being overly apologetic on the telephone, you need to think again.

I myself learned this lesson the hard way. I had been working as a fundraiser for a political campaign (that will remain nameless!) in a northern district of Chicago, when I found out just how vital a strong voice is. My initial efforts involved my idea of "killing them with kindness" and this usually entailed over the top sympathy and empathy with whoever I was speaking with. These two approaches are for the most part, very bogus. No one is going to want to connect to you and what you are offering just because you feel sorry for them, or even worse, they feel sorry for you. So it would be a good idea to cut the sympathy crap and leave your empathy at the door. Because you are trying to encourage people to join your team, not drown in their (or your) sorrow.

During my tenure as a phone bank operator for this campaign, I remember one incident in particular that clearly showcased the need for a direct and unapologetic voice. I had been going through my leads when I came upon a guy that actually seemed interested in being a campaign donor; I thought at last I had found my target audience. But to my chagrin it all fell apart in comically rapid fashion shortly into the call. You see this guy was a dedicated voter in the district and was genuinely interested in the campaign and our candidate. He just had one question; he asked me why my candidate's campaign people had called him up on his cell phone, rather than the work phone he had indicated on previous paperwork as his contact number.

It was a really simple question, but somehow I turned this simple bit of interest into a complex problem in no time flat. Without him even saying as much I immediately assumed that this man was a bit annoyed that we were calling on his cell phone, and so going on this assumption I acted accordingly and immediately apologized for the perceived interference. The man then assured me he didn't mind but offered up the fact that he was just surprised that they had managed to reach his cell phone. Even with his bit of reassurance, I again took the apologetic approach and told him I was sorry for the error, and then made the fatal mistake of adding, "Sometimes this campaign makes a lot of simple mistakes". It was after I let that monster of a proclamation out of my mouth in the name of sympathy and empathy that I wound up alienating a regular client.

The man jumping on this statement of campaign mismanagement the man then politely agreed with my statement and told me that he wouldn't be voting this year, because it just seemed like the campaign didn't have its act together. I then said my brief goodbye and hung up the phone in shock over my single handed, split second destruction of the voting potential of a regular constituent. It was on that day that I learned that being an apologist doesn't accomplish anything. If you behave like you are an intrusion, or allude to and accentuate any perceived flaws, you are only going to alienate your target audience

You should never let on that your product is flawed and should speak of it in only the most glowing of terms. Don't behave as if you are heaping some undue burden on someone else. You should consider your sales call to be an exciting and engaging broadcast. Your goal is to get in and out of their quickly and efficiently, while covering all of the key points of the product. So avoid behaving like an intrusion, and don't get lost to apologetics, just focus on turning your prospective client into a referral.

Another major misconception people have when it comes to formulating a sales pitch that they are overcome with this overwhelming feeling that they are begging. This my friends is all in the mind. It is all about perception and if you act like you are a beggar, begging for attention, begging for time, and begging for a sale, then you will be treated like one. The amazingly simple solution to this then; is to not act like a beggar!

If you open that call up with a sound confident voice without hesitation people will pay attention to you. You won't have to beg for their time if you speak to them in a manner that makes them naturally inclined to listen. You need to part with this begging mentality as quickly as you can and realize that you are not foisting worthless goods on people hoping that out of the kindness of their heart they will pay you for them.

Instead of holding a begging mentality, true entrepreneurs have a service mentality. This means that they realize that they have a valuable service to offer. And they state their case in that manner, that they have a special opportunity of great worth that they would like to extend to their target audience. When you behave in this way, the target audience on the other end will react in kind.

Chapter 3: Crafting Marketing Scripts That Dazzles Your Audience

Everyone wants a good script. From Hollywood producers to cold callers, having a good dialogue is priceless. One of the first tenants that need to be adhered to when delivering scripted dialogue to market a product is to leave the information you are delivering relatively open ended. You don't want to come off as forced in any way, you don't want to tie people down and constrict them too much with your words. People like to have their sentiments and feelings heard, and the more you hear out their own critiques and feedback, the more they are appreciated. Your delivery should be fluid enough to allow for adjustment as it is required as you most likely will be dealing with people of varying communication styles and viewpoints. So make sure you leave some breathing room in your scripts to represent this quality of the marketer/client relationship.

One good example of an open ended script would be one that allows for what is known in the network marketing world as an "elevator speech". The elevator speech, which gets its name by comparing the amount of time it takes to lay down a good intro with the duration of a trip on an elevator, places your intro script at no more than 30 seconds. This means that in half a minutes time you should be able to summarize the nature of your business or product and the key points of how you believe it may be of benefit to your target audience.

The main focus of this brief introduction is strictly two-fold, to present yourself and the inherent value of your proposition. This is your opportunity to explain to potential clients exactly how it is that your product or service can enrich their lives. The elevator script should immediately begin with your name and the name of your company and then immediately after that dive right into what it is that your product or service uniquely brings to the table and why it is that your target audience should care about it.

Try to focus on the unique solutions of your application rather than just blatant features. All of this can be done in just one sentence. Here is an example of an opening line for an elevator style script; "My name is "Blank" and I help people connect with new customers by showing them the most current and most effective ways to promote their business over the Internet". This opening one liner works to introduce yourself, states your intent of purpose and markets your product/ service, all in one breath.

Working a lot like the log line of a film whose job it is to sum up an entire movie in one sentence, the first line of your elevator script summarizes your entire marketing campaign. Once you have developed your one line opener rehearse it constantly until you have near perfect timbre and pitch, because this one line in the elevator script will be the most important part of your sales pitch. Because your presentation of this one line is the first impression that potential clients will have of you and since we live in a world that has a lot riding on first impressions, this one line introduction couldn't' be more important.

After your opening line has been delivered you should follow it up with a series of open ended and relevant questions. Once you have their attention with the opening introduction, it is crucial to capitalize it by fixating their mind on thought provoking questions about their business/situation and what you have to offer them. Some examples of open ended questions would be things like; "Tell me about your business/vendors?" and "Where do you see your relationship with this (insert subject) in the near future?" And another good follow up, "How do you conduct business with (insert subject)?

As you can see these questions are slightly vague, and this is done on purpose, because good follow up questions in your script should not put your audience on the defensive, but should be open ended questions/statements that allow your potential client to think at a leisurely pace about their business/situation in comparison with your service/product without feeling threatened or cornered. And also, in this relaxed style of communication you will be able to glean the most information from your client, than you ever would if they were made to feel defensive in their response.

With enough effort you should be able to craft an engaging opening line in your script, but if you continue to struggle in crafting a convincing pitch you can always turn to someone else to write it for you. If you do find yourself in need of a good script writer you can always check out "The International Association of Business Communicators" there is quite a bit of information about this organization available online and they have chapters all over the country, they are excellent at pairing business people up with script and business writers that will be able to meet their needs. Another option for finding someone to write dialogue for you would be to turn to freelance sites where writers sign on for writing contracts at fixed or hourly rates.

Chapter 4: Turning Leads Into Referrals

The thing that you need to understand leads is that while they may be a means to an end, they are not the final story when it comes to network marketing. Although in the beginning you will find it far easier to generate leads than it is to establish good referrals, leads are really just a short term fix, while it is those solid business referrals that will generate the most turn around in your business.

A referral as the name implies, is someone who was "referred" to your business. The fact that they were referred, instead of you just happening upon them, tells you that these are people that are actively looking for something. They have already checked in with your contact people who referenced you to them, this presents you a very good opportunity to market you and your business as the ultimate solution to whatever this referral's problem/need may be.

Putting your name out their to as many referrals as possible is like a ripple effect in a pool of potential candidates who can be easily transformed into new down line distributors for your business, multiplying your chances with each new referral. Referrals are a wonderful opportunity and usually very receptive to your follow-up with them. Creating a network of these referrals keeps on generating that positive ripple effect in the pool of potential candidates. Good feedback goes a long way and like a series of good feedback nodes, your referrals immediately pick up and generate this positive buzz on down the line, leading your network to rapid sales, growth, and profit.

Turning your leads into referrals will leave a lasting resonance of good will chatter around your company, utilizing the best marketing strategy of all; "word of mouth". And as you begin to routinely round up high quality referral candidates it will be a great promotional tool of your own savvy as a network marketer. Which will ultimately cause those in your immediate scope of business to have even more faith and good will for you, and as a gesture of this good will, they will multiply your referrals even more!

Chapter 5: Learning From The Pro's

All of the ideas mentioned so far in this book are proven strategies for network marketing success. But you really don't have to take my word for it, because the countless testimony of those that have thrived in this system speaks for itself. Just take the example of Barbara Norris, when she began Network Marketing back in 1990 she was a young mother and wife just looking for a way to make some extra money. At first she just networked her products among close family and friends to make a few extra bucks. It was good for a supplemental income but she still had to hold down a day job as a bookkeeper for a Home Depot in Nashville Tennessee.

But in the year 1994 a series of events would occur that would take her from a weekend Network Marketer to a pro in quick succession. It was in that year that Barbara became pregnant with her second child, it was during her maternity leave for her second born that she became determined not to go back to the standard 9 to 5 anymore. And as fortune would have it, along with Barbara's newborn, there was another item in its infancy stages that would be delivered that very same year as well. Because it was 1994 that saw the first introduction of something called the "internet".

That's right, while contemplating her next Network Marketing strategy Barbara had the realization that this new system that was being bandied about as the "Information Super Highway" held out great promise to make all of her marketing dreams come true. This demonstrates a great deal of farsightedness on her part back in 94, because even thought the internet is second nature to us now, back then most people couldn't make heads or tails of it. As was famously and comically demonstrated by the then Today Show hosts Brian Gumball and Katie Couric who appeared absolutely dumbfounded in a 1994 news segment about the invention, with Katie Couric flustered and frustrated asking, "What is the internet?"

But not Barbara, she was one of those rare few that jumped onboard the so called, "information highway" as soon as the roads were opened. And even in the internets fledgling state she soon found a multitude of ways of getting the word out. Truly putting the "Net" into "Network Marketing" she even began building her own rudimentary websites which was quite a feat to say the least, since Windows 95 wasn't even out yet, but this enterprising mama was ready to rock the net out of her with her very own network!

And in the process she became quite good at website design very early on, back when it was still quite a skill to have. She then further networked this talent by getting her friends and colleagues to let her design their web pages, as she built up her resume from this, her referrals began to really take off, and before she knew it she was in demand all over the place for not only designing websites but also for making postcards, greeting cards, business cards, fliers, and many other publication medias, and all of these things while making her a significant profit worked as built in network marketing advertisements that only naturally brought in more leads and referrals to her business. And by the late 1990's she was already making over 10,000 dollars a month with no sign of slowing down. With that many she bought her and her husband nice cars and was able to take her kids to the best schools in her community. Mrs. Barbara Norris is a true Network Marketing success story, and we should all tip our hats to her and what she has accomplished through her pioneering spirit.

A similar success story awaited one very enterprising Network Marketing blogger that goes by the name of "Daniel". Beginning his marketing career in a very modest way, his first venture was to sell beef jerky products, which he marketed online solely through the use of yahoo chat. Not exactly a flashy lifestyle, or something to write home about, just slinging a few pieces of jerky in yahoo chat, but soon the wind would increase in his sails and he would go from barely making anything, to making a fortune.

His breakthrough came after attending a convocation on Network Marketing in Florida, he believed that his meeting of the minds held so much promise for turning his sales around that he dropped everything to hob knob and yes network with these complete strangers in the Florida sunshine. He says that the marketing contacts he met at this convocation not only opened his eyes but opened some very real doors for him. According to Daniel, a big part of life really is "who you know" and this couldn't be more true in the world of Network Marketing, establishing these contacts was key for his success. Just from this one pivotal moment, he has a referral base that will last him for the rest of his life. These are just a few true stories from the Pro's of the business.

Chapter 6: Cold Call Versus Warm Approach

Cold calling or cold scripts are just as it sounds, the idea of reaching out to someone out of nowhere, out of the cold and trying to establish some sort of rapport with them. In today's world of instant information and online social media, it has become rare to have to place a cold call, because for most people the information of a prospective client is just one Face Book or LinkedIn click away. Most of our interactions today would be termed, "warm market approach scripts". As opposed to a cold call approach, a warm approach entails that you know something about the client, you aren't just starting with a cold, complete unknown, there is already dialogue and rapport there, it just needs to be managed and built upon.

A warm sales approach always begins with open ended questions. For example, if you call up the office of some executive somewhere, and his secretary answers the phone to tell you that Mr. Executive is out of the office, don't leave a message, and don't tell them to have the Exec to call you back, instead of all that, you need to start asking some questions of your own, but the key is you have to be quick about it and at all times maintain the warm flow of conversation.

So if the secretary says he isn't in the offices, use a warm follow-up question, and shoot back, "Do you keep his calendar?" You see, this is a good warm, positive and open ended questions and one relevant to who you are speaking to, the secretary. Any secretary or receptionist in their right mind would have their boss's calendar! So using this follow-up question immediately opens the door to further dialogue instead of being shooed away by a bored receptionist.

Utilizing this warm approach will most certainly get a positive response such as, "Why, yes, of course, I'm looking at his calendar right now!" and this extends to you an invitation to further cement your proposal, whether the Exec is in the room for it or not. This is your time to shine, just stay upbeat and confident, sound as though you are meant to be there, and you will be treated accordingly.

Don't say you are selling anything, but just mention the proposal in a business professional manner, a good demonstration of this, while the secretary is still browsing the calendar is to tell him/her something like this, "Good. I'm glad you have access to his calendar. This is John with Enterprise Financial Systems and I'm calling to schedule a 15 minute discussion with him. I plan to accomplish this no later than Monday of next week. I have availability Thursday afternoon and in the morning on Friday and Monday. What time works best for him?" With this little display you have presented your case quite warmly and effectively and now you are through the gateway to reach this client.

Just like with any relationship there needs to be room for growth, once you have your target audience in mind find what it is that gets them really energized, what gets them really inspired and jump on it. In the above mentioned scenario as soon as the caller realizes he is dealing with a secretary whose job it is to organize and familiarize themselves with their bosses schedule, the caller immediately flows into that subject matter. This is the entire basis of the warm approach to calling and marketing. You can think of warm calling as a nurturing approach that builds confidence in the receiver that you have something of value to offer and by that you immediately build interest in the subject matter. No matter what you are selling or service you are offering the warm approach can do wonders.

Chapter 7: How to Net Your Network

Some aspects of online network marketing have already been mentioned in this book, but the subject is so important that I wanted to include one final chapter solely devoted to crafting an efficient marketing presence online. Because in today's digital world, if you do not have a proper online presence, a digital representative of you and your business, for most of the world you do not exist. If you are not utilizing online media in today's market you are losing about 75 % of your potential clients.

One of the best ways to corner that online market is to have your own personal website that specializes in your product or service. When designing a web site the number one thing to keep in mind is who your target audience is, and once this is established, cater the site accordingly. This means that you should be using web advertising, e-mail campaigns, directory listings, and squeezes pages that fit the profile of who you are marketing.

To utilize web based marketing you need to keep your content relevant to what your clients want and make the page easily accessible based upon what their search habits are. This means that in order for potential customers to be able to reach your page you will need to optimize your search engine potential. Known as SEO (search engine optimization) this is an extremely useful tool to get traffic on the internet. SEO is the process of placing keywords on your site in such a way that any relevant search made by a potential customer will send your page to the top of the search results page.

Search engines work by running automated software that use programs to crawl the Net. These programs then detect and gather pertinent information from websites and then spit back that information to the engine's database to be analyzed. The web pages that most closely line up with search engine logic will then line up as the top ranking hits in the results page. Because search engines are regularly reprogrammed one of the best things you could do is to periodically check up on web site analytics to have a grasp on just how it is that people are using your site. A proper user analysis should include; peak usage periods, visitors, pages, views, usage patterns, and purchasing conversion rates. Also be sure to interpret, analyze and review all potential back-end data you have.

Once your search engine is optimized you want to also tweak your site to where the right section of content appears in the link provided by the search engine. For example, if you have a site dedicated to sporting goods, but someone is searching specifically for baseballs, then you would want their search in the engine to bring up a link directly to the baseball section within your site.

To do this you will need to utilize what is known as "landing pages". Landing pages like the name implies, work to "land" the person searching within the engine to the appropriate content they are looking for on your site. To have them be able to pull up the exact category saves people a lot of time, and of course, in the marketing business time is money, so the more time you save a potential client when browsing your site, the more likely they are to use your services. So taking the time to imbed landing pages within the search would be an excellent idea to promote business within specific niche markets within your site.

Now that we have spent some time talking about using direct websites as online promotional tools, lets talk about the more indirect approach of social media. I say "indirect" rather loosely, because although social media platforms are not direct domain names of the product, hitching a ride on Face Book, Linked and Twitter can still rise to and even sometimes eclipse the marketing power of a direct website of your product. The great thing about social media is the fact that they are, well, inherently social!

Just think about it. The whole world is using Face Book nowadays and once you have a powerful Face Book page with your product and you start getting tons of friend requests every day, this is instant free marketing and like a snow ball effect your referrals just build and build until you have an ice mountain of a fan base for your product. Every single person who friend's your products Face Book page is an instant advertising and marketing tool for your business, this is truly Network Marketing in its most true sense.

Special Bonus

To thank you for purchasing my guide, I have specifically prepared the bonus **"Operations Quick Money – Step by Step Guide to Your First $100"** report for you. This report will show you how you can start generating some residual income from your internet marketing endeavors.:

In this report, you will find:

1. How you can use the internet to generate residual income

2. Effective techniques to find highly profitable products to promote

3. How to drive web traffic for free

3. And Many More…

To access this special bonus, simply visit the URL below:

http://bit.ly/2kC8Ia2

Conclusion

More and more, everywhere you go you hear of Network Marketing, and if you just take a look at Amazon, the site is absolutely flooded with "self-help marketing" books. This being said, with so many books to choose from on this topic, you are probably ready to ask, "So what's so great about this book?" and "What does it have that others do not?"

Well the reason that I call this book the, "Direct Sales Bible" is because it doesn't try to throw you a sales pitch, it doesn't promise things that it can't perform, it just throws out all of the facts in one comprehensive book.

Throughout the pages of this book you don't find much filler but you most certainly find a lot of facts. Being able to take advantage of Network Marketing is a skill that you have to learn in order to be successful, this book offers you all of the best tips, strategies and ideas to get there, but the implementation of all of these concepts will only work if you put forth the effort to make them work. This book is merely your guide, we don't try to persuade you one way or another, and how you proceed is up to you.

If you use the script examples provided, take on a warm approach as highlighted and network your tail off as directed, there is really no reason why you can't become an amazing Network Marketer in less than 30 days. This is not a guarantee but rather an observation and a promise. Just buying this book won't do it for you, but buying this book and taking all of the information provided to heart will. If you truly utilize all of the methods outlined in this book there is absolutely no reason why you can't become a Network Marketing Rock Star and I'm glad that the content provided in this book has helped you to obtain that role.

-- Ken Chong